# Turning 50
## ...And Other Reasons to Laugh

### By
## Danny Jones

*Turning 50 ... And Other Reasons to Laugh*
by Danny Jones

Printed in the United States of America.

ISBN 9781498479103

Scripture quotations taken from the King James Version (KJV) – *public domain*

Back cover photo courtesy of Ex Nihilo Media

Cover design by Allyson Lyons

www.xulonpress.com

# TABLE OF CONTENTS

# DEDICATION

The hair is a little thinner. What hair remains is a little grayer. The ears are not quite as keen as before. The eyes take a little longer to focus.

But you and I are still here!

It's been an interesting journey, these past six years. It was in 2010 that my very first book entered the marketplace, and you embraced the content enough to want the second book, and even the third.

If you're reading this, you've also taken home the fourth book of my ramblings because — hopefully — you enjoyed the first three enough that you wanted this and you didn't accidentally buy it because you thought it was a book of cute animal pictures.

So, this book is dedicated to you, the reader of *Turning 50 ... and Other Reasons to Laugh*. Thank you for being a part of my life.

# FORWARD

W ell, he did it!
My good friend Danny Jones turned 50 in 2016 (the year this book was published).

The timing was perfect, too, since this was the first year Danny would have been old enough to write a book that is titled *Turning 50...and Other Reasons to Laugh*.

Danny and I have been friends for many years. Though we currently work together at *Singing News* Magazine, we were friends long before either one of us were associated with the magazine.

Danny has always had the unique ability to find humor in just about any type of situation. Since he has spent the better part of his career traveling and representing *Singing News* at music events across the country, he has not only made lots of friends but has also experienced enough "stories" to fill several books. In fact, this is his fourth book.

And speaking of traveling and representing *Singing News*, I should point out that this year marks Danny's 21st year with the magazine. He is still on the road about 42 weeks out of the year and, at the time of this writing, has personally logged more than a million miles in the last 21 years.

That is an impressive track record.

This wonderful collection of stories is only a sampling of the stories—true stories—that have happened to Danny and some of his friends in the Gospel music field. As you probably already know, the *best* stories are those "real-life" events we can actually tell on one another and laugh with each other about.

I am very honored to have been asked to write the "Forward" for Danny's new book. Since we are dealing with the subject of getting older, I wanted to list a few things that Danny can now look forward to, now that he has turned 50. After all, he's never been this old before.

You know you have turned 50 when...
- You realize that you are now able to hide your own Easter eggs.

- You can order the AARP membership card, and start receiving a discount at restaurants.
- You notice that, along with your discount card, you also receive smaller portions of food at those same restaurants.
- You sit in a rocking chair and can't get it going.
- The clothes that you've put away until they come back in style... come back in style.
- There's nothing left to learn the hard way.
- You finally know all the answers but nobody asks you the questions.
- Your joints are more accurate than the National Weather Service.

In all honesty, turning 50 isn't all that bad. Just turn the page and let's find out why...

Rick Francis
Operations Manager
*Singing News*
Member of the "50 and older crowd"
June 7, 2016

## Chapter 1

# I Just Want To Say

The year this book is being written is the year I turn 50. Half of one hundred...Fifty percent of a century...Five decades.

While some people may dread turning 50, I've actually somewhat enjoyed it. First, I now get senior discounts thanks to organizations such as AARP! (Fellow 50 and older members of society just smiled because they enjoy that little perk of aging, too.)

But now here comes the biggie: Turning 50 means that I can now get a free pass on some of the things I say (listen to those seasoned hands applauding!). You know what I'm talking about—those little things we say as we get older and bolder because we have a bit of attitude since our patience is beginning to wear thinner than our hair. Because I'm not as *young as I used to be, I'll now be lumped into the "he's-old-enough-to-say-what-he-wants-to" group or the "bless-his-heart-he-can't-help-it" crowd. Either way, I win!*

*So, now that I'm in the "50 and Older" division, I have some things I'd like to say. You may have said a few of these, too...*

1.) If I don't clean out my closet for five more years, I'll have it made because I'll have more clothes that have come back in style than that are out of style. I'll even have money left over for a senior drink at a fast food restaurant.

2.) I'm at that age now where I can accurately tell you the weather forecast without looking at TV... or an app...or just by looking out the window. Frankly, if I get up in the morning and nothing hurts, I wonder if I died during the night.

3.) I've been cleaning some things out of my office. Thus far, I've found three previously unreleased Elvis Presley songs, a chicken recipe with the name "Sanders" written at the bottom, and what appears to be about 18 minutes of reel-to-reel tape in a box with the notation "R.N. White House." There's hardly a person under 30 who'll appreciate any of that, but maybe I'll get a few bucks in a yard sale.

4.) During my five decades of living, there have been many incredible inventions. Some are truly mind-boggling with their greatness. On the other hand, one of the world's worst inventions is the dreaded "SPORK." Believe it or not, the first patent for this frustrating and maddening combination of a fork and spoon was issued in 1970. I so wish the patent office had been closed that day.

5.) It was on Nov. 19, 1863, that Abraham Lincoln delivered the Gettysburg Address.
One hundred fifty three years later—and despite what a few of my smart-aleck friends (*read Michael Booth* and *Mike LeFevre*) say—I want to point out that I was *not* there.

6.) Not all senior moments are bad. For example, there is that moment when you remember your hotel key is on the other side of the door that you just closed.

But...

There is also that moment when you see the extra key that you put in your car's console yesterday. *Us "seasoned" people are smarter than we look, aren't we?*

7.) Do you remember the good ol' days when we all thought, "If I can just get out of school and into the real world"? Now we're more likely to think, "I didn't realize how good it was to just worry about homework." But publicly, you can bet I'll just tell the kids what it was like to walk to and from school, uphill both ways in the snow...

8.) Recently, I was in Texas and an elderly gentleman told me I reminded him of Harry Truman. Yes, that Harry Truman. Short...Pudgy...Balding... Harry Truman.

Harry's last year as President of The United States was 1953. He may have been a fine president—*BUT I DON'T KNOW! I WASN'T BORN YET!*

I may be 50, but apparently I look like I'm 97... oh, just never mind. I'm still mad.

9.) In 1972 Gene Cernan was the last man to walk on the moon. Some scientists believe that his footprints in the dust may still be undisturbed after 44 years.
That's nothing. I've got dust in my brain that's not been disturbed in 50 years.

10.) This comment is for the 20-something kid who wanted to know how I lost my hair. *Well, Spanky, scientists say that the earth is spinning at approximately 1,000 mph. Hmmm. Guess that's why my hair looks blown off! Go play in your sandbox, you whippersnapper.*

11.) Have you ever had one of "those" days? But just like the sturdy ol' horse in the field, I'll keep plowing.
I may kick someone like the sturdy ol' horse does, but I'll keep plowing.
*(Wow...some of y'all just gave me a standing ovation!)*

12.) A representative of the HOA of the subdivision I live in just knocked on the door and asked for a donation for the community's swimming pool. Do you think two glasses of water was enough? To those people who like to disturb our naps for things that really don't affect our lives at all, let *that* be a lesson!

13.) No, irate "my-kids-can-do-anything-they-want-to" parents, I'm not sure *you* should be angry when the restaurant manager comes out and asks you to keep your kids from playing on the dining tables while you and your friends eat in the next booth. If the manager doesn't do something, a few "50-something's" might take things in their own hands and teach the meanings of "yes, sir" and "no, sir."

14.) Now that I'm 50, I don't feel too embarrassed by being passed by that woman with flowers in her hair and who is still living in the 1960's and driving a SmartCar. Oh, sure, I'd still like to run her off the road, but I'm not as embarrassed as I would have been when I was 49.

15.) I just sold a lawn mower on Craig's List. That's the last time my neighbor wakes me up on a Saturday morning!

16.) I read somewhere that there will be a surplus of fruitcakes during the coming holiday season. Interpret as you may.
And by the way, I've not suddenly developed a fondness for fruitcakes just because I've turned 50. So don't mail me any. If you do, I may save it and throw it at you the next time I see you.

17.) Because I'm always being told I forgot some-one's birthday or that I should have sent a card or a present, let me just remind you that, yes, I know I'm not always the greatest at telling everyone "Happy Birthday" on his or her birthday.
So, since we now live in a "politically-correct-don't-want-to-hurt-any-feelings society," let me wish "Happy Birthday" to anyone who has had a birthday in the past 12 months or will have a birthday in the next coming 12 months. Today is inclusive in either category he or she may choose.

There. That should do it.

18.) Some people amaze me. Some astound me. Some leave me speechless.
Then there are those that cause me to believe there is life on other planets—and some escaped and moved next door to me.
*Yes, I'm destined to be the old man who sits on the front porch and yells at the kids to stay off my grass.*

19.) More than likely, I will not be any smarter when I wake up tomorrow.
Don't *even* think about commenting.

20.) Just because I stand in the grocery store looking helpless while comparing dietary fiber supplements, no one needs to feel compelled to ask me how I'm feeling. Someone asked me the other day if they could help me, so I gave them the most honest answer I could: Many have tried and all have failed.

21.) As I get older I realize there is a very, very fine line between stupidity and, well, everything

else. In fact, "the difference between genius and stupidity is that genius has its limits."
That quote has been attributed to Albert Einstein, even though there's no credible evidence he actually said that. However, the accuracy of the actual statement has been proven time and time again.

23.) My list of contacts in my phone used to be listed alphabetically by first name. I can't do that now because I'll never get out of "D": Dr. Smith, Dr. Brown, Dr. Hall, Dr. Matthews...

24.) Now, at the age of 50, I've come to grips with the fact that some of the words that come out of my mouth will be forgotten as soon as they pass through my lips. That's why there was no Number 22. I couldn't remember what it was. *You just went back and looked, didn't you?*

25.) As my job includes lots of travel and thus many restaurants, I've noticed something on hundreds of menus that puzzles me. Just when did macaroni & cheese become a vegetable?

26.) Been thinking.

That should scare the daylights out of you.

27.) Finally, if Yogi Berra were alive today, he'd understand the simple honesty of this daily truth: Sometimes getting to tomorrow is a 24-hour ordeal. Someone say "Amen."

**By the way...**

Back when I thought anyone 50 or older was ancient, I used to watch older men gather at a local restaurant early every morning and just sit around a table to talk. I wondered what the big deal was.

Now that I'm 50, I have to wonder if the world would be a better place if more people did that.

You can say "Amen" again.

## CHAPTER 2

# ENCOURAGE. GIVE. LEAD. BE KIND.

*B* *ob Crawford writes "The View From Here"* *each month for* Singing News. *It's an enter-taining mixture of Southern Gospel music and real world life, done in a way only Bob can share.*

*Bob is one of those guys who would be perfect for those early morning meetings I just mentioned at the end of the previous chapter. He's witty, he's smarter than he thinks he is—and he's been around long enough to have insight that comes only from life experience.*

My entry into this crazy world of Gospel music was not glamorous, nor by being "discovered." Oh, I *was* discovered—but not for being the good tenor singer I thought I might have been. If anything, I was discovered through a comedy of errors.

Like many other times in my life, I had said yes to a volunteer position to which I had no business saying yes. It was a hot summer afternoon in Waco, Texas, and I had agreed to umpire a girls' softball game in a local church league. I wasn't very good in the first place and I certainly didn't know that an umpire had much control of the flow of a game.

The Head Umpire—of the whole league, no less—called me over to the fence between innings. As I would find that he was capable of for many years to come, the suited-up-decked-out-in-all-black head umpire smiled as he politely chewed me out for letting the game run late. Then, after the game, he again reminded me of my errors—only this time, he wore a million-dollar smile, coupled with a giant handshake and an almost fatherly half hug.

The umpire's name was Marvin Norcross.

Two weeks later, my part-time quartet opened a church service for The Galileans, an outstanding group that had just signed a recording contract with Waco's Canaan Records label. The president of that company was standing against the back wall of the packed little church. Somewhere in the second chorus of my solo on "The Lighthouse" (that's the one I'm pretty sure I was doing better than Vestal Goodman could have—yeah, right!) my eyes connected with that record company president.

I remembered that million-dollar smile but I unfortunately forgot the lyrics.

Later, I got another big handshake and a shoulder-to-shoulder hug. In our conversation, I explained that I worked a couple of jobs, but that I was mainly an all-night disc jockey at a country music radio station near Waco.

That record company president was Marvin Norcross.

Two weeks later, I was sitting in an old block AM radio studio and transmitter/tower building, in the middle of a cornfield outside of Waco, working my all-night shift. It was unnerving, to say the least, when someone knocked on the metal door. I reluctantly opened the door, only to find not one, but two, million-dollar smiles. There stood Marvin Norcross and his beautiful wife, Chic.

Oh, he also had a 45-RPM record of Wendy Bagwell's "Here Come The Rattlesnakes."

Little did anyone know what those meetings on the ball field, the church, and the radio station would bring into my life.

Three months later I was the very first radio promotion guy for Word Music/Canaan Records.

What *did* those meetings bring? How about fast friends, via a comedy of errors on both of our parts? How about a career that could be summed up as "having once worked for Marvin Norcross"?

Be encouraged, as you never know how a chance opportunity or a seemingly innocent meeting may affect your life. Sure, it brought me into a career that I loved dearly but the years of working with Marvin Norcross that resulted from those meetings taught me the importance of being an encourager.

Of all of life's lessons, and the many famous "Norcrossism" quotes, I can honestly say that my life verse is based upon Romans 12:8: If your gift is to encourage others, be encouraging. If it is giving, give generously. If God has given you leadership ability, take the responsibility seriously. If you have the gift of kindness, do it gladly.

Encourage. Give. Lead. Be Kind.

## CHAPTER 3

# HE MAY HAVE A POINT

*N*othing is as interesting as real life. And somehow, life has a way of making you appreciate "the little things" as you get older. It can make you laugh just as easily as it can make you cry. Somewhere in between the life lessons, the laughs, and the tears are the thoughts that make you say, "You know, he may have a point there." And, of course, none of these really hit home until we have many days behind us...

1.) Always remember: The guy who sat next to you in the restaurant and made railroad tracks in his mashed potatoes while you laughed at him just might be the brain surgeon you'll need next week.

2.) There comes a point in time that after you've said all you can say, done all you can do, and given example after example, that you just have to let someone pull the TV off onto his or her head so they will learn.

*But, alas, some go through six...seven...three hundred televisions.*

3.) You know all those goofy kissy ducky faces that seem to dominate photos now?

That means that somewhere down the road a lot of people are going to be asking *what was I thinking?*

4.) I'm beginning to believe that thinking before opening one's mouth is a lost art.

Likewise, thinking might be a lost art, too.

5.) Today's cars are so advanced that they can drive down the road without human assistance, park next to a curb without the driver turning the wheel, activate the windshield wipers automatically with the first drop of rain, and much more. But the license plate is still held on by screws that were designed long before any of us were born.

Sometimes simple is all you need.

6.) If you have to brag on how good you are, are you really that good?

7.) Have you ever noticed that the ones who complain about a problem the most are often the ones who have created the problem?

8.) You know that filter that is supposed to be between the brain and mouth? Some people need to change their filter because it is obviously too clogged to work.

9.) Always remember that if you hide behind the works of others, the day you find the others gone is the same day your lack of ability sells you out.

10.) Need a challenge in your life? Find a shopping cart with smooth round wheels!

11.) Just remember that history started out as the future.

12.) Opinions are better when there are facts behind them.

13.) Definition of a successful person: Someone who can smoothly fold fitted sheets—without losing his temper, saying ugly words, throwing the sheets across the room, balling the sheets up and just sticking them in the bottom of the drawer, getting frustrated to the point of tears, or just giving up—back into the original packaging.

14.) Fuel prices go up in the summer because of refineries having to prepare "summer blends." Then prices go up in the winter because refineries have to prepare "winter blends."
Sounds to me like we need more spring and fall blends.

15.) Unwritten Rule of Life No. 63: The overwhelming majority of the people who gripe about how you do your job and always say *I could do that better* have never actually done that job nor have the inclination to try it.

16.) A friend told me the other day about a horrible dream he had. He dreamed that Krispy Kreme was turning into a health food store.
*That's not a dream—that's a nightmare!*

17.) Someone once said the more you do *something* for free, the quicker people expect *everything* for free. And when *everything* is free, the value of *everything* is *nothing*.

18.) When looking for the Achilles heel, people tend to look too low. Look higher—to the chip on the shoulder.

19.) Many like to collect certain things. Personally, I like watches. It is not an obsession but I will stop and look at a watch closely if something catches my eye. Some collect old cars, baseball caps, model trains, old soft drink machines. You get the idea.
Meanwhile, I'm convinced my clothes dryer is a sock collector.

20.) Life lesson #32: Never scratch your nose while attending an auction. You can't afford it nor will you have anywhere to put it. Trust me.
I never wanted to own a full metal old English suit of armor. Lightning storms have taken on a whole new meaning around my place. But I will admit that my television reception is incredible!

21.) You know those days when you just want to beat your head against the wall because you're convinced intelligent life form is not out there? *I'm running out of wall...*

22.) I just saw a Facebook post that said, "Stuck in traffic jam in Idaho."
*Traffic jam in Idaho?*
*Idaho??*
*Really???*

23.) There's nothing like the joy of reaching into your suit jacket and finding a $50 bill. Unfortunately I've only heard about that joy.

24.) If I could just be the person my dogs think I am I'd be awesome.

Apparently, greatness only depends on my ability to provide doggie treats.

25.) Words guaranteed to strike fear in your dating teenager: We found your baby pictures!

26.) This perfectly describes my golf game at age 50: I hit a hole in one! One swing. One window. One hole.

27.) Oh, how I wish some people would remember this before speaking to others: If you don't know, don't assume.

28.) Need a challenge in your life? Find a shopping cart with smooth round wheels!
*(That was No. 10 on this list, but it was worth repeating! Besides, we over 50 have a tendency to repeat ourselves.)*

29.) No one on this side of eternity will ever have all of the answers.
If we did, there would be no need for faith...or the promise of a better tomorrow.

30.) This "point" blew me away the first time I read it—
and still astounds me every time I consider the
significance of these words. Charles Spurgeon,
without a doubt, spoke from his heart when he
said, "While others are congratulating themselves, I have to lie humbly at the foot of Christ's
cross and marvel that I am saved at all." Amen.

# CHAPTER 4

# THE LADY ON THE RADIO

*S*inger Lauren Talley is one of my favorite persons, even if she is 17 years younger than me. But as she once told me, she's an old soul trapped in a young body.

*How does that happen to someone? Life, that's how. Lauren has had her share of ups and downs but over time God has shaped her into being a person with maturity that comes from being spiritually grounded—and open to His direction.*

*Answers. We all want answers. And we all want them immediately.*

*Likewise, we want that promise of a better tomorrow. We want encouragement. We want hope.*

*But where do we find it?*

*Lauren has the answer.*

I love music. I was raised in a Gospel singing family, with whom I still perform. Music has shaped my whole life, personally and professionally. I love lots of different types of music but, since I'm around it so much, it might surprise you to know that when I get in my car I usually don't turn on any music. Rather, I am a huge fan of talk radio, and I listen every day. I listen to several different shows with varying viewpoints.

And sometimes I talk back to the radio. *Don't act like you don't!*

When I'm not being educated, at least I get a good laugh. But today was no joke.

Today I sat in a drive-thru line listening to a caller express her frustration and pain to the host. She had recently lost her father; her husband had lost his job (and the family's health insurance), and the bills were mounting quickly. She didn't know how they were going to make it. The exhausted, frightened lady said through her tears. "I just get so depressed. It seems like there's nothing to hope for anymore. The world is so scary now. I'm afraid for my family. No one seems to have any answers. Who's going to save this country and this world? Where is our hope?"

I nearly spilled my large sweet tea as I heard myself shouting at the radio...

I KNOW!!!

*For unto us a child is born, unto us a son is given: and the government shall be upon his shoulder: and his name shall be called Wonderful, Counsellor, The mighty God, The everlasting Father, The Prince of Peace. Of the increase of his government and peace there shall be no end, upon the throne of David, and upon his kingdom, to order it, and to establish it with judgment and with justice from henceforth even forever. The zeal of the Lord of hosts will per-form this.* —Isaiah 9:6-7

God is in control of this world. He created it, He owns it, His will orders the stars and planets. Nothing happens in this world that He doesn't allow, yet sometimes He's a hard One to understand.

Why does a loving God let God-fearing people get cancer? Get divorced? Lose a child? Lose their life savings? Why doesn't He stop horrific acts of violence? Where was He when that horrible thing happened?

*God, don't You understand how I feel?*
Yes, He does.

*Surely he hath borne our griefs, and carried our sorrows...But he was wounded for our transgressions, he was bruised for our iniquities: the chastisement of our peace was upon him; and with his stripes we are healed. —Isaiah 53:4-5*

He's been there, too. He felt your pain at the cross. He didn't just feel something similar to how you feel, He felt the very pain you feel now. He felt the unbearable pain of living a broken, sin-stained existence, and He died for it.

We still live in a broken world, but we who have a white-knuckled death grip on our faith in Jesus Christ can and will overcome.

*...fixing our eyes on Jesus, the pioneer and perfecter of faith. For the joy set before him he endured the cross, scorning its shame, and sat down at the right hand of the throne of God. —Hebrews 12:2 (New* International Version)

*And I heard a great voice out of heaven saying, Behold, the tabernacle of God is with men, and he will dwell with them, and they shall be his people, and God himself shall be with them, and be their God. And God shall wipe away all tears from their eyes; and there shall be no more death, neither sorrow, nor crying, neither shall there be any more pain: for the former things are passed away.*
—Revelation 21:3-4

If I could answer the lady on the radio I'd tell her to cling to Jesus like He was everything, because He is. If you feel like the lady on the radio, I'm praying you feel the peace that comes from knowing that He has overcome the world. One day we will rule and reign with Him forever and until then, we can live fearlessly with Him.

## CHAPTER 5

# MOUTH 1, BRAIN 0

*I* *n the first chapter of this book I mentioned that I*
*would now be included in one of two categories*
*of people, one of them being the "bless-his-heart-*
*he-can't-help-it crowd." This will explain why...*

I learned an important lesson today: Apparently
there are some words that are just inappropriate for
certain places.

Let me explain. Today I was headed out of town
and I dropped by the bank to withdraw a few dol-
lars for traveling expenses. As I drove around to the
ATM, I saw a technician working on the machine.

Now you've probably seen the same scenario
many times. There he was, with his big bag of tools
on the ground, and he was hunkered down in his

work. In fact, the whole scene reminded me of an old black and white gangster movie—you know, where the guy is trying to crack the safe and he's hunkered down in his work and there's the big bag of tools on the ground next to him.

Anyway, since the ATM was not an option, I parked my car and walked into the lobby so I could get the money the old fashioned way—from a teller. I was greeted by the sight of three or four people in the line of each of the three tellers who were working that day.

I wondered why the atmosphere seemed a little tense but I soon learned that the bank's computer systems were down and nearly everyone in line was there for the same reason I was.

Little by little, the lines shortened as people gave up waiting. But since I was okay on time I kept my place and, by the time the computers were beginning to come back online, I was at the head of the line. Patience pays off sometimes, you know.

The teller that day is someone I've seen in that bank for years. In fact, all of the tellers that day were. They know me on a first-name basis. So when she asked, *What can I do for you today, Danny?* I was just my normal self.

That's when I discovered that sometimes being your normal self doesn't pay off.

With that black and white movie still playing in my mind, I said, "Yes, since your ATM out there is being robbed, I came in here to get some cash from my account."

Not one person on that teller line heard any part of that sentence past "being robbed."

Heads looked up, cash drawers started slamming, and I heard people running in the offices behind the tellers. If there had been a security guard on duty that morning, I'm sure I would have heard the sound of a gun magazine being clicked into place, and I would have been nose to nose with the floor tile.

I must have looked like Barney Fife or Goober from "The Andy Griffith Show" trying to get everyone calmed down!

Fortunately, I've not had to change banks.

Yet.

## CHAPTER 6

# THE DAY I BECAME A VETERAN

N ow that we've established that everyone makes mistakes, I'd like to share with you something that I have always found funny.

What you are about to read is something I can picture myself doing—and now that I'm 50, the odds are greatly increased that I'll do something similar before too long.

Barbara Huffman is another of the great writers of Singing News. She's well respected for integrity in writing and she's known throughout Southern Gospel music for being one of the genre's best friends.

But what I really like about Barbara is that I made it to 50 years old before I did anything like this! By the time she turns 50, she may have topped this...

I consider myself as patriotic as the next person—maybe even more so, since I have four family members who have served or are currently serving in the United States Air Force. I have a huge respect for the U.S. military and those who willingly offer themselves for our freedoms and protection. I can assure you there is no way I'd ever intentionally disgrace or interrupt a ceremony honoring our beloved military veterans.

Note the key word in that previous sentence—*intentionally*.

I'm not sure what year this was, because frankly, I've tried to block the whole incident from my memory. But it just seems to keep rearing its ugly head, especially since our fearless leader at *Singing News* loves to keep reminding me of it.

As a feature writer for *Singing News*, I sometimes attend concerts where our editor-in-chief, Danny Jones, is representing the magazine. Translation: Danny sets up a product booth and sells magazine subscriptions to fans at the concert. I assist him in sales at these events—particularly when there's a crowd of customers or he has to leave the booth to go to the stage to tell about the magazine or emcee the program, as he often does. This is the general

set-up for the evening I'm going to tell you about—
the day I became a United States Veteran!

We'd had a particularly "mad-house" type of
rush at the table that Wednesday evening, the first
night of the annual Brumley Gospel Sing. There
were literally several lines of people trying to sub-
scribe to the magazine and get to their seats before
the concert started. In the hullabaloo of the moment,
a credit card was inadvertently left at the *Singing
News* booth. Danny said one of us needed to go to
the stage, have the emcee announce the person's
name and tell them to come pick up their card.
Because he was still busy with people and I was
sort of the "floater," if you will, I told him I'd go.

It was about five minutes before the program
was to start, so I began making my way to the
stage. The doorways and aisles were crowded with
people and it was hard to make my way through. We
were moving in the general direction of the stage,
although I couldn't see a lot in front of me having
not been blessed in the height category. I honestly
thought it was that last minute crunch for people to
get their concessions and find their seat before the
concert started.

I'm not sure when I discovered that I was the only woman in a line of men slowly making their way to the front of the auditorium. At some point, I realized people were applauding wildly. I looked up and realized I was not in a disorganized sea of people trying to find their way to their seats. Instead, this was an organized parade of sorts, four very distinct lines of men walking proudly in a formation. Some were waving in appreciation to the crowd. I saw a few wiping their eyes. One of them was carrying a very large American Flag.

The light bulb was slowly beginning to come on by now, but it wasn't bright enough yet. I said to myself, "This group of men is headed to the front of the room. I'm headed there, too. I wonder what we're all going to do when we get there?"

Then my dear friend, Mr. Bob Brumley, affirmed — from the stage, no less — what was unfolding before my eyes. "Let's hear it for our veterans! Let them know you love them. We even have a WWII vet here tonight!"

Have you ever seen someone do a U-turn in the middle of a crowd of people? A complete 180? Let me put it in military terms for you. It's called an "about-face." And I did one about as quickly as any human has ever done an about-face in his or her life. I tried to look inconspicuous but when one person gets out of formation, it's fairly obvious—especially when people are trying to shake your hand as you walk and saying things such as "God bless you for serving our country," or "You're a real hero," or "I hope my daughter grows up to be like you," or, Danny's personal favorite, "Were you in World War II or The Korean War?" I'm not as young as I used to be but I'm *not* that old!

You've heard of draft-dodgers. You may have read about or even know a conscientious objector. I'm neither of those. I'm just a girl who blunders into the Veteran's line and demonstrates the "about-face"—in front of several thousand people.

That's what it was, you know—a real live demonstration of a military marching drill maneuver during the ceremony to honor the veterans. You know that's what it was. Right?

For some reason, I don't think you believe me.

Oh well. God Bless our veterans—and me, too!

## CHAPTER 7

# LIFE ON THE ROAD, PART 1

*I*'m not sure how it happens. Perhaps it is just *a sheer numbers thing—I travel frequently, log enough miles, stay in hotel after hotel—and eventually the odds catch up to me. Regardless of how, the end result is the same: After 50 years—and most of them spent on the road—there are some things that you just can't make up...*

It's late, nothing to eat after the concert but drive-thru stuff. I get to the speaker, place my order, and after the cashier repeats it she asks, "Is this for here or to go?"

Umm...

Language barriers can often be a detriment during a hotel stay. But sometimes even language doesn't come into play.

To prove my point, here is an actual conversation between a hotel maid and me one morning in Myrtle Beach, South Carolina, as I walked out of my room door to get a bottle of water from the vending machine. Before I begin, though, keep in mind that the very first thing I do when I go into a hotel room is hang the "Do Not Disturb" sign on the door knob.

Maid: Do you need room service today?

Me: No ma'am. I would put out the "Do Not Disturb" sign but I don't have one.

Maid: I will bring you one when I clean your room.

Me: But, ma'am, I just told you I don't need the room cleaned.

Maid: Then you should hang the "Do Not Disturb" sign on your door.

Umm...did I miss something here?

## Speaking of "Do Not Disturb" Signs

I've been involved in Gospel music so long that I really can't remember when I crossed the threshold into its hallowed ranks. By my guess, that's been more than 36 years ago—WOW! Thirty-six years...432 months...13,150 days...315,600 hours... you get the idea.

And a gazillion miles.

Because I've spent the majority of my adult life "on the road," I sometimes forget that some people are just the opposite: they just don't travel. It's because of that little fact that one of my most memorable travel incidents took place on the last day of a 1,400-mile, two-day run.

On that particular trip, I was accompanied by a friend who had never ventured far from home. Nonetheless, he wanted to "get out" a little and see some of the places and events he had heard me talk about. Just to be completely honest, my friend had never stayed in a hotel until that trip.

After driving all night after a Friday concert, we checked into a hotel. Unfortunately, there was no time to rest as we had to hurry to the venue, set up the table and be ready to go when the doors opened.

Frankly, I was exhausted...running on fumes... struggling...throw in all those terms you can think of. All I could think about—and all I really wanted— was just to sleep. Even though it was a large crowd and a strong sales night, I couldn't wait for the concert to be over.

Naturally, this concert was one of the longest events in Southern Gospel music history—well, it sure seemed that way!

After returning to the hotel and settling in for the night, my friend climbed into his bed while I did the accounting of the night's sales. In seconds, he was snoring.

I will confess at this point, my opinion of him was not very high.

After I finished my work, I went to the restroom to brush my teeth and get ready for bed. As I made my way to my bed, my friend stirred over in his bed and muttered something that could have been "Goodnight."

I said "Goodnight" and as a quick afterthought, I added, "Did you put out the 'Do Not Disturb' sign?"

"Yes, I did," he said. And with that I started to lie down.

As my body was moving into that horizontal position that you get into when you're about to get in bed, he muttered "And I almost never got that thing to stand up, either."

Still, until this very day, I don't think I ever touched the bed. I think I actually caught myself in mid-air and immediately returned to a standing position.

"What did you just say," I asked.

"I said, 'I almost never got that thing to stand up.'"

And then he started snoring again.

*Surely he didn't*, I said to myself.

I went to the door, opened it, and sure enough, there was no "Do Not Disturb" sign hanging on the handle.

Instead, it was right there on the floor, propped up against the doorframe.

## Chapter 8

# SMH

*Now that I'm past my 50th birthday, I've realized that there are more things than ever that cause me to SMH. In case you don't know what SMH is, SMH is the current Facebook/Twitter/all other social media abbreviation for "Shake My Head." Things I see in the news, hear on the radio, read online, or even see in person are increasingly causing me to wonder about the sanity of the human race.*

*But, in all transparency, some of those things do give me a good laugh...*

As I write this, I'm having routine service done on my SUV. The woman sitting across from me in the waiting area at the dealership has been complaining about the windshield wiper blades on her 2011 vehicle falling apart. The technician just came by and asked, "When did you last change the blades?"

The woman's response?

Wait for it.

"Change them? You're supposed to change them?"

SMH.

Then there was yesterday. I actually uttered something I thought I'd never hear myself say to a cat: *Turn. The. Dog. Loose.*

SMH.

*(In all fairness, there were cat treats and a hungry dog involved, so I guess that helps explain the situation.)*

Here's a little story from a recent trip. Have you ever stayed in a hotel and it seemed as though the people on the floor above you were stomping grapes?

I was in Monroe, Louisiana, when this light bulb came on in my head. See, I'm amazed at the number of people who travel with their pet elephants. Apparently there is also some type of regulation which mandates that people with pet elephants must stay in the hotel room right above mine.

SMH.

*But little did I know things were about to get even more interesting.*

When daylight arrived, I walked over to the nearest restaurant. Because of the early hour there were just a handful of people there. At the table next to me was a young family, and the parents were trying to explain the significance of December 7, 1942. I thought the woman was doing well in her explanation until one of her kids asked, "Where is Pearl Harbor?"

What happened next caused me a real dilemma. I asked myself: *Should I clean up the chocolate milk I just spewed across the room myself or call the waitress over to do it?* Then I realized I had yet another dilemma if I eventually shared this story—I would risk making many of my friends such as Mark Trammell, Pat Barker, Bob Sellers, and a few others, really mad. In the spirit of the late, great newscaster Paul Harvey, here is the rest of the story. As for my friends, they'll get over it.

The woman, who was wearing the red University of Alabama sweatshirt, told her kids that Pearl Harbor is just off the coast of Texas.

SMH.

*(Well. Ok. This could be a problem. But then again, what's 4,000 miles over the course of history?)*

SMH. Again.

This one, however, probably takes the cake. It is direct from the "some things you just can't make up" department...

I was at lunch a few weeks ago when I overheard these words: "We can't get married. I can't afford to change my tattoo."

SMH.

Let's do it again.

SMH.

One more time just for good measure.

SMH.

At least when it comes to SMH, I know I'm not alone. Larry Riddle of The Primitive Quartet is one of the most humble and genuine persons I've ever met. His soft-spoken manner has endeared him to thousands and thousands of people around the world. When someone compliments the quartet or him personally, he bows his head in gratitude and thanks the Lord for the kindness of others.

So you can just imagine the scene that day at Hominy Valley—the 40-plus acre singing grounds in Candler, North Carolina, where the quartet hosts two multi-day events each year—when a gentleman walked up to Larry and began sharing with him in 100% complete honesty.

"Brother Larry, I just wanted to tell you that earlier this week I drove all the way to Pennsylvania, and then the next day I drove all the way back from Pennsylvania."

"Well, bless your heart, friend. That's a lot of miles to cover in just two days."

"Yes sir, it is. But I wanted you to know that I listened to The Primitive Quartet's new CD all the way up there and all the way back."

"You did?"

"Yes sir, I sure did."

"Well, brother, that's very kind of you to say that. I hope it blessed you."

"I never could figure out how to get that CD out of my player, so I had to listen to that thing all the way up there and all the way back."

SMH.

Let's throw in another for Larry...

SMH

And...

This morning—for the very first time in my 50 years—I actually felt tall!

Then I realized the clothes rod in the closet was sagging.

SMH.

## CHAPTER 9

# I LOVE (HATE) FACEBOOK

*S*ince *I brought up SMH as a product of the online world in the last chapter, I think it is time I made a confession: I have a love-hate relationship with the Internet—and most notably, Facebook. Sure, it makes my job easier as I have immediate access to thousands of reference tools; I can connect with others instantly and I can see things from around the world that I might not otherwise ever enjoy. I love that part.*

*What I don't like is how quickly the Internet became a place for some people to display their "nasty" side with insults, character assassinations, rumors, and flat-out lies.*

*And I'm not talking about just the politicians, either!*

*I'm not the only one with this type of relationship with this electronic monster we can't live with or without. This is something that has affected all ages—not just us, the great "50 and older" bunch.*

*Despite your relationship with the Internet, I feel certain that you too have experienced a few moments like these...*

There are days when I am convinced this is a true statement: The Internet is an electronic system by which some people prove their ignorance.

April Fool's Day makes an annual ONE-day appearance. Based on some of the stuff I see on Facebook the other 364 days of the year, I'm not 100% sure everyone got the memo.

Just being on Facebook does not make you an expert at anything. Only life's experiences certify you.

If "thinking before you type a post on Facebook" was a required skill for a job or for advancing a career, I'm afraid some people might have a real problem.

People read those things, you know.

Somewhere along the way "expressing themselves" got confused with "stupidity."

A phrase no longer used in a sufficient quantity: Grow up!

Some people should think before posting to Facebook. Some should think twice. Some should think three times.
Many should just keep thinking.

You know that "Most Recent" tab on Facebook? The one that, after clicking it, will bring up the most recent posts from your friends so you don't have to wade through tons of stuff that you've already seen? I was thrilled when I discovered that little tab—so I clicked it.
My Facebook page refreshed—you can probably imagine how anxious I was, just knowing I was going to see the latest!
I started seeing posts from yesterday...and the day before...and the day before that...
Hmph. Really?

I clicked "Most Recent" again.

It got worse.

I remember thinking *Guess I'll have to refresh again tomorrow to see what happened today.*

*Or should I say yesterday today even though it won't be yesterday until tomorrow. Or should I just wait until the day after tomorrow so today's tomorrow will be a yesterday that happened the day before yesterday on the day I want to see now?*

SMH. Wait, wrong chapter. Facebook confuses me on a daily basis.

By the way, not long ago I heard someone say "no one writes in a diary any longer."

Yes, they do.

It's just called Facebook now.

I will admit that I find some of the most enlightening things on Facebook. I just saw one nugget of wisdom that read, "Sumo wrestlers don't make the best jockeys."

While I would say the accuracy level of that statement is quite high, I just never thought that would be one of the first things I would ever read on a Saturday morning.

You know all those quizzes that you see there on Facebook? It is simply amazing how much I've learned about myself—*even if it is wrong!* For example...

1.) I belong in a state that is 1100 miles away — but only on days that are either before or after any Tuesday.

2.) The DNA quiz suggests I have the same molecular structure as broccoli or silly string that's used at birthday parties.

3.) My career path should have been muffler-bearing polishing with a cactus-watering business on the side.

4.) My favorite color suggests that I was once the ruler of a country that I can neither spell nor pronounce.

5.) The third letter of my first name, seventh number of my Social Security number, the punctuation mark at the end of the 28th sentence I wrote four days ago, and the last two letters of my 2nd grade teacher's grandmother's third cousin's ex-mother-in-law's maiden name indicate I will be an underwater-basket weaving instructor before I die.

*I know beyond any shadow of a doubt that this is wrong because my 2nd grade teacher's grandmother's third cousin is still married to her second husband.*

6.) Because I live in a state that contains both vowels and consonants, I'm likely to be run over by an Amish family in their handcrafted buggy while they are on the way to the International Conference Of Electricity.

7.) The numerical equivalent of all the letters in my name is all the evidence needed to demonstrate that I'm allergic to paint, bees, pancakes, asphalt, polyester, nails, elephants, acorns, cotton candy, bluebirds, major league football, and air.

*I can safely say this is more evidence that these quizzes are inaccurate. I have no problem whatsoever with cotton candy.*

8.) My driver's license number has enough of the same numbers found in mathematical formulas used in nuclear physics to cause, when properly used, internal combustion within the earth's core—but only in a location exactly 2.17 miles from the right side of the northern edge of the little green sign facing the sun at the intersection of six streets in a city who's name begins or ends with any of the alphabet's first 17 or last 9 letters.

9.) The combination of my first name, the last name of a person in Texas, the name of that Texan's dog, the name of the coach of Italy's national professional quilt sewing team, and the last three ingredients of my shampoo prove that I was either Abraham Lincoln, Charlie Chaplin, or Marilyn Monroe in a previous life.

*See, I told you all of this stuff was wrong.*

10.) Finally, because Facebook quizzes say I have no knowledge of automotive terms, my animal personality equates to that of a dyslexic squirrel, I know all the state capitals, *and* I can answer not less than, but equal to, and not more than, one question concerning the history of midget mud wrestling in lower Alabama, I will lose lots of hair by the time I'm 60.

*Wait...*

*Uh oh.*

## CHAPTER 10

# LIFT ONE ANOTHER UP

*W*e all need encouragement. We all need laughter. We need to be able to navigate through life armed with things that help us endure the non-pleasantries that so often are thrown at us. The people that can help us most during dark days are often the ones who have been there. Sheri Easter knows...

Thirty years ago, during one of the first interviews that Jeff and I did, the interviewer asked a question that had never been asked of us, and impromptu, we answered in exactly the same manner. He asked, "What is the purpose of your ministry?" It was a question I had never contemplated because the answer seemed too easy to assume that the purpose of Gospel music was to tell others about Christ and offer that hope to a lost and dying world. But something about the *way* he asked the question made us both answer with the simplest of words, "to encourage people who are hurting," we replied.

Jeff and I had both been broken people when we first met, although we were broken in very different ways. I was an overachiever who volunteered for everything, worked non-stop at my job and gave 150% to my college classes. I was determined and driven to make a difference. I loved God with all of my heart and was waiting for Him to lead me in whatever direction He chose, but in the meantime, I was making every moment count, preparing myself for the future. I wasn't aware at that time even the 'best laid plans' could crumble.

Jeff is a free spirit with a knack for making everyone laugh! He was assuredly the class clown and chief mischief-maker. He loves people and loves to be surrounded by them. He lived his life in the moment and never thought much about the future until he made the decision at 18 to marry. A year later, he became a father for the first time and 15 months later, welcomed baby number two.

Jeff and I were walking different pathways that were leading us the same direction.

On June 12, 1984, I heard the news that changed my world. After a weekend of finals, I drove home from college and my mama met me at the door with the news of my daddy's sudden and unexpected death. It was the Tuesday before Father's Day and every plan that I had made crumbled or was immediately put on hold.

Jeff is kind and trusting, and about that same time, now at the age of 24, he was doing his best to make a new life for himself without allowing the roots of bitterness to creep in after a failed marriage at the age of 20. He had trusted and been let down by life and everything in it and getting back up was much harder than he had anticipated. We were both broken and searching desperately for a way to heal.

We met at a Gospel concert and started a conversation that hasn't stopped. It was warm, honest and a safe place to lay the broken pieces. We began to heal by breathing in, breathing out and trusting God to do the rest. It wasn't easy and it wasn't quick, but it was worth it to come out on the other side restored.

When we say that our purpose is to encourage others through our music, it is because we both have needed that encouragement when we were most broken. On the surface, the brokenness isn't always easy to see, but there is something about the healing in the words of a Gospel song that peel the layers away revealing the raw places that need a healing balm. Every song we choose, we do so from a place of brokenness, hoping and praying that the song will encourage someone else. The Bible tells us to lift up one another, to edify and encourage, bearing ye one another's burdens. It is an admonition that we take very seriously and accept with open arms knowing that many people offered us words of encouragement that brought us to this place of restoration. Be slow to judge and quick to encourage, you never know when you may be in that place of need.

# CHAPTER 11

# LIFE ON THE ROAD, PART 2

Remember that old saying of "no good deed goes unpunished?" You know the one—about how trying to help someone turns around and bites you?

Several years ago, I was on a trip with The Booth Brothers. This was during the days when Ronnie and Michael would share in the driving chores.

Well, mostly Ronnie.

As we were headed across eastern Kansas late one night, Michael was driving across endless straight stretches of road. I was sitting in the buddy seat and we were, as people say, "solving the world's problem."

After about two hours and four bottles of water, Michael said that a restroom stop would be just what the doctor ordered. But despite little traffic and straight roads, there was nowhere to easily pull over so that he could run back to the on-board restroom.

But that's no challenge for those people who spend most of their days on the road. Just call someone up to the front to take the wheel for a few minutes. In other words, change drivers while still rolling down the highway.

So, Michael called out Ronnie's name. There was no response. Then Michael called out his dad's name (Ron, Sr., was doing some driving during those days). No response from him either. I opened the curtains that separate the driver's area from the rest of the bus and looked back. Everyone had apparently called it a night.

So, Michael looked at me and asked if I'd take the wheel while he went to the restroom.

Considering that I've spent a lot of time behind the wheel of a bus, I agreed. So I took the wheel.

And drove a mile or two, thinking that Michael would soon be back. Then I logged in another five miles. Then 10 more.

Not only had Michael gone to the restroom—he had also gone on to bed!

I parked the bus 6 hours later at the next venue.

And when I climbed into my bunk, Michael was getting out of his. And he asked, "So, whatcha been up to lately?!?"

There is one more part of this story that I should share. Apparently, I've not been the only one to witness Michael's disappearing act. It turns out that his dad has had a similar experience.

Many years ago, after The Booth Brothers had gotten their first bus, the group was traveling across Florida early one morning. The sane brother, Ronnie, had been driving for several hours when he pulled off the road to get Michael up. Michael had just gotten back on the highway when Ron came to the front, looked through the windshield into the wee hours of a Florida morning and asked, "How are you holding up, son?"

Michael replied, "I'm doing OK. Kinda beat, though."

Ron said, "Well, pull over and I'll drive."

Soooo...Michael did! He didn't even drive a whole mile! Ron got in the driver's seat and drove the rest of the trip.

And, Michael went back to bed!

It was only after Ron retired from road life that Michael told his dad what happened that day. And, in case you're wondering what Ron said to Michael, let's just say it involves phrases such as "never too old to be put up for adoption," "I should have left you on the side of the road," and the really good one, "I think the judge will understand."

Friends and relatives are not the only ones who can play tricks on you and leave you hanging. Mother Nature herself has been known to have a mischievous streak.

Had you been reading this the weekend I first recalled this story, most of the country was experiencing shivering temperatures as sleet, snow and other wintery precipitation dominate the newscasts. It was during this same weekend that many Southern Gospel artists lost their entire slate of dates because of weather-related issues ranging from snow/ice accumulation to extreme cold to burst water pipes. It's been a while since weather cancellations have been so extreme, but as any group who has lost dates will tell you, one time is plenty enough.

But what happens if bad weather moves in *while* the event is taking place? More than one concert attendee and group has been surprised when they've walked outside following a concert only to find that the parking lot is iced over or the snow has covered the sidewalk.

That's fairly minor, though, compared to being at an outdoor sing—and watching it snow.

It's happened to me twice. Once was at Hominy Valley (Candler, North Carolina) at The Primitive Quartet's annual Fall Sing. Yes, I said "Fall." This was in mid-October and what had been a mild month was erased that weekend as a quick-moving cold front pushed through. People in the audience were bundled up with layer upon layer of clothing, and at first glance the scene reminded me of a convention of Eskimos. When the audience applauded after each song, it sounded like a big pillow fight.

Let's be honest—it is a little odd to be at an outdoor sing and watching snow accumulate on the edge of the stage...the sound equipment...*the audience*. But believe it or not, those 800 people stayed for the whole event.

It might have been that they stayed because they were frozen to their lawn chairs. Still, the point is, they stayed.

Truthfully, this abnormal snowfall didn't faze me because by then I had seen it all. The one that takes the cake for me was that bone-chilling night in Boone, North Carolina, at The Greenes' annual event they used to promote at the fairgrounds. This was in *August*, folks. You know, August—as in typically "the-hottest-month-of-Summer -and-you-can-fry-an-egg-on-the-sidewalk-*August*." For most of the week leading up to that day, the weather had been Chamber of Commerce perfect. But then that picture of loveliness was tossed completely as there was a 45-degree drop in temperature in one day.

And there, behind the stage in the western mountains of North Carolina in early August, Tony Greene and I watched as snow started falling. He looked at me; I looked at him.

In perfect unison, we said, "Snow?!?"

Then he said, "Well, I've learned my lesson."

"About what," I asked.

"I knew I should have ordered sweatshirts for the table. I'll have 'em next year, you wait and see."

Normally, I'd say that was good planning. There was one small hiccup. The hottest August in anyone's memory hit Boone, oh, about 365 days later.

Backstage, Tony and I both recalled standing in that same spot the year before watching the snow fall. He looked at me, grinned, and said. "Shut up."

He didn't even have to ask what I was thinking!

Then he said, "I'll save 'em until next year. It *will* get cold again someday!"

## CHAPTER 12

# DEFINED BY STRENGTH

*I*f you're thinking Michael Booth is an awful person for those unbelievable, terrible, horrible, hideous, grossly-outrageous—I'm trying to think of every word I can to build sympathy for me—things he did to me and his dad, don't worry. He's already forgotten about them, and Ron and I are just about over it.

*Almost.*

*Well, we're getting there. And since both his dad and I are now over 50 we feel less remorse for any future action we may take as we plot our revenge on Michael. It is truly okay.*

*All kidding aside, it would have been easy to get angry—but why? We know Michael's heart and it shines way above his practical jokes. Sometimes you have to look way past the surface to truly under-stand—something Daniel Ball of The Ball Brothers knows first hand...*

Don't know why I'm sharing this...maybe it will help someone. Many people that only know me through The Ball Brothers probably don't know that I have a really hard time being around crowds of people. No joke! Sometimes I get so nervous that I feel like I'm suffocating and look for the nearest door to escape. I've left grocery stores because too many people lined up behind me. I've left restaurants without finishing my food because all the tables around me filled up. My idea of a vacation is going anywhere with my family that we don't have to be around any crowds of people. My wife and kids are great and help me out tremendously. I'm not anti-social—I love to talk to people (in smaller group settings). I have a lot of great friends but most of them know that when it gets crowded, I'm gone. Fairs, malls, airports, and sporting events are all places I try to avoid because of the crowds.

So you might be wondering, "If you have some crazy fear of crowds, how does that work out with singing?" It doesn't. This is my weakness. When

I'm in my own strength, I can't even walk into a crowded building. I pray for strength in this area a lot. I cannot do what God has called me to do on my own.

I think it's awesome that many people don't know this about me. That's a testament to God's strength in my weakness. Your weakness doesn't have to keep you from your calling. It may be the key to God working through you. Don't be defined by your weakness; be defined by His strength.

Second Corinthians 12:9-10 says *And he said unto me, My grace is sufficient for thee: for my strength is made perfect in weakness. Most gladly therefore will I rather glory in my infirmities, that the power of Christ may rest upon me. Therefore I take pleasure in infirmities, in reproaches, in necessities, in persecutions, in distresses for Christ's sake: for when I am weak, then am I strong.*

# CHAPTER 13

# WHIPLASH

*You can observe a lot just by watching. — Yogi Berra*

S orry for the whiplash you've just experienced. As you've noticed, I try to make each chapter flow right into the next one by tying thought together.

But since there is no way I could do a new book without including a few references to my hero, Yogi Berra, and his way with words, I had to find a place for this short chapter.

So here it is. No segue, no tie into the preceding chapter, no nothing. *Wham!* It's just right here.

Sorry about your neck.

My family and friends have on more than one occasion told me that I can invent the craziest words as I get tongue-tied. They've also reminded me that

I can make a mockery out of the English language as I mispronounce words and string together sentences that shouldn't go together.

In other words, they think—no, wait, they *know*—I'd make Yogi Berra proud. If you don't know who Yogi Berra is, tell your grandkids to Google him for you.

So, in honor of that great filet'er of words and thoughts—and because I've included some of my "Yogisms" in previous books—I now share with you a few *new* things I've said.

You probably be doing your own version of SMH after this...

During the past 10 years, I've been living through 120 months.

A work in progress is like a work that is still being worked on.

Every now and then I have a great idea. Unfortunately, this is not now and it won't be then either.

If it doesn't rain today, chances are it's gonna be a no-rain day.

If that doesn't light your fire, your wood is not going to burn.

Yes, I said all of those things.
*Publicly.*
Don't judge me.

## CHAPTER 14

# REAL LIFE IS FUNNY

*I*'ve said it hundreds of times: nothing is funnier than real life. Maybe it's just me but as I get older, I find the funny things of real life to be more humorous than anything you could make up.

*One of my "Over 50" friends, Aaron Wilburn, understands this phenomenon. And another "Over 50" friend, Karen Peck Gooch, well, she lives this phenomenon.*

The other day I was talking on the telephone with Aaron Wilburn. As per the course of nearly all of our conversations we always ask, "What city are you in?"

On this particular day, I was in Normal, Illinois.

The other end of the line grew silent—and then Aaron burst out laughing.

"You? In Normal? You and *normal* just don't go together in the same sentence."

After I finished complimenting Aaron on his height (he's one of the few people that I am taller than), he said, "I've got a newspaper clipping around here somewhere that has a wedding announcement from the newspaper there. It talks about a man form Normal marrying a woman from Oblong, Illinois. The headline reads, "Normal man marries Oblong woman.""

Not too long ago I was in Memphis, and after a long day of meetings, I found a quiet little restaurant on the edge of town. At the table behind me were two police officers discussing their work. I didn't mean to listen in on their conversation but since their conversation was much more interesting than the soccer match (between two countries I've never heard of) that was showing on the restaurant TV, it was hard not to.

It was a good thing my mouth was empty when one of the officers said, "I'd rather fight a riot alone, blindfolded, and unarmed than get between the store doors and a 70-year old woman with a cane on Black Friday. At least I *know* what the *rioters* are gonna do."

Then there was the day I was working at my desk and my cell phone buzzed. It was a text message from Karen Peck Gooch.

Since Karen and I work closely on several projects, a text message from her is not unusual. But this one? Well...

It was a grocery list, with the note to check the date on the eggs.

Obviously, it was a mistake. But do you think I could resist letting it go?

*Noooooooooooooo.*

I sent a text back: *I've checked every egg in this store and there's not a date on a single one of them. What do I do now?*

She's still never responded.

By the way, this is not the last time you'll hear from Karen in this book. In fact, I've saved another Karen story—probably the greatest one of all time—for a later chapter. Don't jump ahead and spoil the surprise, though.

This chapter would be a good time for a "kids say the darndest things" moment. You've probably heard this before, but it is like being 50—it's an oldie but a goodie. Just think about this old story the next time you're sitting by your favorite munchkin...

The morning church service had just concluded and after making their way back to the car, a mother and her son were talking about the service.

In reality, the mother was complaining about the service.

"That ol' preacher! He stomps and snorts all over the platform. He's too loud and scares the babies and makes them cry. His sermons drag on and on. And not only that, did you hear that choir up there? Oh my goodness! Have you ever heard such singing? Everything they sang was slow and not only that, those people just can't sing."

After a few minutes of pondering what his mom had just said, the young boy looked at her and said, "I thought it was a pretty good show for just a dollar."

## CHAPTER 15

# CHANGE OF PERSPECTIVE

*I*f you're over the age of 50, how many times have you been asked this simple, yet somewhat annoying question: Do you feel any different?

That budding sassy senior citizen within us—well, at least the one in me—wants to respond with, "No, I've always felt with my hands, so I'm not going to do anything differently."

But since that's not the Christian thing to do, so many of us respond with the typical "I feel the same" answer.

That may be true for most of us. But let's be totally honest: There's something about turning the calendar into that second half century that causes us to have a different outlook on things. I'll give you an example...

As this crisp sunny Saturday morning begins, I watch in silent amazement as a leaf breaks loose from a limb and twirls to the ground. As it rides the breeze down to the ground, I follow it's progress until it meets the earth's surface—not with a crash, but with softness as though it landed with the guidance of a pilot's steady, yet gentle hand.

*That younger, dreamed-filled version of me wrote that. This next part comes from the realistic senior-discount laden guy at the end of the street...*

Then I watch in horror as 23 million more leaves follow it, using my yard as a parachute leaf-landing zone—just like the leaves from my neighbors' trees are doing. The leaves that have gathered in the cul-de-sac have found their way to my driveway, and the breeze that has now escalated to gale force speeds blows them against my garage door—which means as soon as I open the door those leaves will blow inside, laughing at me during every inch they slide along the floor and tucking themselves into corners and behind things that will hide them for months, possibly even years.

*Since you liked that one, let's try another...*

This morning I stood at my window, gazing at the blanket of cold white that had covered the ground in a perfect layer. The quietness of the moment seemed to suspend the hour. A thin stream of water had frozen in time as it had fallen from the mailbox. In the distance I could see smoke as it drifted from someone's chimney. I watched as someone lumbered through the snow, heavily bundled in winter attire, yet faithful to his routine.

As I stepped back from the window that allowed me to see this natural art, my mind was overwhelmed with a solitary thought...

You know, there's something to be said for living near the equator.

CHAPTER **16**

# WHO PUT ALL THESE TREES HERE?

*E*ven though I was experiencing what I'm about
to describe well before I turned 50, I'll never
get used to this one thing: Brain burps. You know,
where you can't see the forest because of all the trees.

How many times have you've been guilty of fit-
ting that statement perfectly? Every now and then,
all of us overlook the simplest things that we've
known forever. This, of course, leads to another
time-tested saying: "If it had been a snake, it would
have bitten me."

Such is the case with Hovie Lister, the legendary
pianist of the great Statesmen Quartet. In an issue of
*Singing News*, I asked the trivia question: "Besides

The Statesmen Quartet, what other professional Southern Gospel quartet did Hovie Lister play piano for?"

The correct answer, as indicated at the bottom of that page, was The Palmetto State Quartet. The problem is...that wasn't the only correct answer.

*Who put all these trees here?*

You see, Hovie played for several quartets during his lifetime. There was that little group of legends (James Blackwood, J.D. Sumner, Jake Hess, Rosie Rozell, etc) called The Masters V. That group was on the road, oh, for about eight years.

So...we have The Palmetto State Quartet and The Masters V as correct answers to that question.

The only problem now is...well, those are not the only correct answers, either.

*Man, those trees are getting thicker.*

Hovie also served at the piano bench for the following groups: Rangers, LeFevre Trio, The Homeland Harmony Quartet, The Sand Mountain Quartet, The Lone Star Quartet and The Lister Brothers Quartet.

And, just for good measure, let's add the fact that Hovie also played for noted evangelist Mordecai Ham and even accompanied C. Austin Miles (remember "In The Garden"?) for a brief time while still in his teen years.

Now, folks, I knew all of this—*I've known it for years*. In the particular case of The Masters V, I attended one of their very first concerts—and I was there the night at NQC when J.D. told the members of Masters V to turn around, and then he re-introduced them as the new Stamps Quartet.

And I knew about Hovie's past with the other groups I mentioned earlier, too. I've read all the history books, listened to the old-timers share stories of those days...and worse yet, I have listened as Hovie *HIMSELF* told me tales of those glorious years.

*There are way too many trees here!*

Folks, I had a full-fledged case of "DUH." If I had been on trial for being smart, there wouldn't have been enough evidence to even get close to a conviction. Despite all of that information being stored in my brain for years, did my brain bother to display the "hey, it's over here" sign? *Nooo...*

To top it off, I'm too young to be able to claim it was a senior moment.

Wait...

I'm 50. Maybe it *was* a senior moment, after all!

CHAPTER 17

# THANKSGIVING—
# FROM THE 50 PERSPECTIVE

I remember well the Thanksgiving holidays of my childhood...the get-togethers, the meals, watching the parades on TV.

I'd still like to be along the streets of New York to watch that department store's parade in person. My family wouldn't let me go, though, because they fear I'd get tangled up with one of the persons holding a control rope on one of those giant balloons and I'd embarrass the whole family because I'd be floating away on national TV while holding on to Snoopy. (How's that for a run-on sentence?!?)

Their resolve is maddening when I tell them "you have no faith in me." Just because I once caused a trombone player to run into a tuba player when I dropped my trumpet in a high school parade? That is no reason to anticipate a problem in a parade in a completely different state.

That could be considered profiling, you know.

Anyway, last year during the Thanksgiving holiday, I read literally thousands of posts on Facebook as people go through their own "30 Days of Thanksgiving." I saw the commonplace—thanks for the Lord, family, friends, jobs, churches, cars, dogs, cats, and so forth—and the not so common (the most unusual was a pet rock named "Stoney"— you can't make this up—someone had been given as a child).

But what I saw the most was "thankful for my salvation." And I must agree with their sentiments.

For all of my life, I've been hearing "we're living in the last days." I can remember my parents saying it, my grandparents saying it, hearing my grandparents say they heard their grandparents say it...you get the picture. You've heard it all of your life, too.

While Scripture plainly states that no man knows the time of His return, Christians—as a group— seem to be coming into more agreement that the hour is drawing nigh. As such, the importance of the Great Commission grows as each day goes by.

We may have experienced our last Thanksgiving, or, it might be the first of 100 more. What truly matters, however, is that whenever the last Thanksgiving of our lives takes place, we know that we are prepared to spend the next one in His presence. And, on a rare serious note from me in this book about the humorous side of turning 50, let me say that as I get older, thoughts like these become more urgent as I think about those who don't know the Lord.

So on Thanksgiving Day—or any day for that matter—when you're checking off the things you are thankful for, check to see if "Thankful for Salvation" is on your list. If it is not, take the time to learn why so many are thankful for salvation and how it will be the most important decision you will ever make.

**PS:** *IF* you watch the Thanksgiving parade, there's no need to look for me. It turns out the folks up there heard about that trumpet thing and…well…

## Chapter 18

# I'm Just A Human Bean

Greg Davidson is a good friend of mine. Canadian by birth, American because he lost his passport while in the states and Canada won't let him back in. I'm just kidding! Anyway, Greg is an American by choice, and he is an illusionist who has used entertainment to get the Gospel message across to people who might not otherwise hear it.

He's also an expert on Barbeque.

Anyway, he's also in the "Over 50" club and like many other members of that club—he's learned that sharing is a good way to get through life. Read on and see what I mean...

Little doubt lies within the acknowledgement that giving is good; everybody knows that. What continues to make me smile is that the shades of giving taste a lot like lima beans. They taste kinda funny, kinda dry at first, but if you give them a chance (and a layer of butter), they're good and more importantly, (at least according to my mom) good for you. I used to despise lima beans but the fact was, I just had to get to know them a little better.

Sure, I was brought up learning that giving and sharing was good but before I ever shelled-out one bite of candy, a single marble or one hockey card, I made sure I had doubles in the other pocket; and I had better be getting something back soon, or the deal was off. It was like the old days of the great white north—a beaver pelt in exchange for a haircut and some chipped beef. It was the way of the north, the way of the west and the way—way past that. "I'll give, but what am I going to get in return?" Had I known, the giver and the receiver were often one in the same party, I surely would have opened my clenched fingers and said, "Here, take." I know for sure, you could have had my lima beans.

Heed this as either warning or promise, but Forrest Gump in a manner of speaking, told us that when we pull on the end of the satin bow, and lift the lid off of life's box, "You never know what you're gonna get." He could have added, "But it will melt in your hand if you try to keep it to yourself." My God-given talents were the things that I demonstrated, displayed but had never truly given; at least from the heart. I had invested so much in my career, in my daily life but so little in eternity. Could my gifts make any significant eternal difference? I decided to try another spoonful and answer the call I had heard from God when everything seemed dry, bitter and hard to swallow.

God always seems to be "waiting up" for me. He's always right by the phone "just in case" and I've found Him not only a good listener but an even better teacher. God has encouraged me to give what I already have and to realize, all I have was His in the first place; it never was mine. Often, my giving seems far too small but God graciously uses it, puts it into the circle and allows the doors of my heart and mind to swing a little further open. Finally, God teaches me to open my arms and my fingers to receive with the same spirit, heart and love He personified and to invest the gifts that ultimately come from whom all blessings flow back into the circle. It's true—you reap what you sow, whether lima beans or gifts from God. And the giving…the receiving…it's like butter!

## Chapter 19

# Life On The Road, Part 3

*T*his chapter is just for those people who think the concert and road life is always glamorous.

Several years ago, after a New Year's Eve eve (yes, that's correct) concert in Gainesville, Georgia, my family and I headed southwest to Atlanta (about 50 miles from Gainesville) to catch an early Saturday morning non-stop flight to Baltimore, Maryland. Once we arrived in Baltimore, we'd drive about two hours to Lancaster, Pennsylvania, for one of Garden Spot Promotions' annual New Years banquet concerts.

Garden Spot actually promoted two concerts on that night—one at Yoders Restaurant and the other—where I was at—at the Shady Maple Restaurant.

Those of you who have faithfully kept up with *Singing News* will recognize that restaurant as one of *Singing News Editor Emeritus* Jerry Kirksey's all-time favorites. Both events were sold out—and that's not bad at all when you consider that the tickets were $43.00 each. That included a meal and the performances of three groups.

Back to Baltimore for a moment. Have you ever been standing in the baggage claim, watching the bags go around and around on that endless conveyor belt and never seeing your luggage? Not seeing even any luggage that looked like yours?

When I checked with the luggage office, I was told it might be in on the next flight. So we waited.

Nothing.

Not only had I not seen my luggage since I checked it in on Saturday morning, *no one* with the airline could even begin to tell me where it is... or was...or where it might be. Nor did anyone even attempt to make a guess at it.

*It was a non-stop flight, y'all. NON-STOP. The luggage would have never had a chance to get off the plane for a quick bite in the terminal!*

By this time, we had no choice but to head on to Lancaster. I had the notion that we might stop and buy clothes along the way, but it seems as though many stores opted to close early on New Year's Eve. Imagine that...

Long story short, I was the Master of Ceremonies at a very nice banquet and I had on the same things I flew into town wearing: blue jeans, a hooded sweat-shirt and my favorite pair of tennis shoes. My family was dressed equally nicely as me.

On the program were The Old Time Gospel Hour Quartet, The Anchormen, and The Hoppers. Claude offered to take me shopping as long as I held the cost down to $10.00—and he even offered to pay half. But I gently reminded the aging singer that the stores were closed because of the holiday.

*Hmmm. Now that I'm 50, Claude doesn't seem that old after all.*

After we got the program off and running, Jason Funderburk (then with The Anchormen) loaned me a few clothes to get me through the evening. Now, Jason and I are close to the same size—but not exactly the same size—and that led to a few interesting moments. I did have to stuff tissue in the ends of his shoes to keep them from slipping off. It also appears that Jason has longer legs than I do, so I kept stepping on the ends of the trousers.

It was either that—or pull them up way beyond my waistline. If I had done that, I would have looked like an old man.

*By the way, I have noticed that turning 50 years old causes one to constantly reach to the top of one's pants and pull them up.*

Nevertheless, the rest of the evening was just fine. So, thanks, Jason, for your kindness and generosity.

Here's the rest of the story...

When we flew back into Atlanta the next day, I was told by the airline that the luggage appeared to be in California and that *IF* they could get it back to Atlanta, they would then ship it to me.

*IF they could get it back? You flew it out there, didn't you?? Why not fly it BACK???*

*You're sensing some of that "over 50 sass" from me, aren't you?*

About a week or so later, Fed Ex dropped off a huge package at my office.

But wait, there's more...

I was told during a follow-up call that the luggage *never* left Atlanta on New Year's eve.

*Never.*

That's my last SMH.

For now.

## CHAPTER 20

# AND THEN THERE'S BOB

*I*f you have read any of my previous books, you
know that if it were not for Karen Peck Gooch,
there would have been several empty pages. Perhaps
it's just the fact that we live a few miles from each
other and our paths cross often ... or ... perhaps
we co-host a TV show together and we're working
together in a studio frequently ... or ... perhaps it
might be that the rest of the people on the Karen
Peck & New River bus immediately pick up a cell
phone and let me know when Karen has delivered
one of her infamous "Karenisms" to an unsus-
pecting audience, but whatever it might be, Karen
has unintentionally supplied more fodder for my
books than any other person.

*But even I was surprised at what transpired after Karen sent me a text one day to let me know one of our mutual acquaintances who had helped promote a few groups in his time—Bob Kilpatrick—had passed away.*

*Before I begin, I need to point out that this story includes a minister who's in Las Vegas to help plant a new church. I know you're thinking "Suurrrrrree he was" but it's the truth! There were also a tremendous amount of circumstances that would have had to happen at just the right time—so much so that if any Las Vegas gambler had taken the 1-to-1,000,000 odds, that person would now be probably be the world's richest person.*

*The minister in this story is Rev. Bill Stacey, another person you've met in my previous writings. He still has, by the way, the notes and photos from his trip if you want proof that he was actually helping start a new church. Bill was also an acquaintance of the dearly departed.*

*So, now you have Karen, Bill, and me. After us three, I will now change all the other names to protect the innocent—that would be just about everyone, including the deceased—but not the guilty.*

*That would be Karen.*

Shortly before lunch on an early Spring Monday, Bill and I received a text from Karen that read ... *Hey guys. Just got a text from a friend that said Bob passed away.*

I responded with ... *Kilpatrick?*

Karen: *Yes.*

Bill: *Really? What's the name of the funeral home his daddy's funeral was at? They may have his obit.*

Karen: *His body is at Smith, Johnson, and Brown.*

Bill: *I'm in Las Vegas looking at church planting. This area is incredibly without a Christian witness. When is the funeral?*

Karen: *Not sure. Praying for you out there. He's going to be promoting groups in Heaven now.*

While these texts had been going back and forth, I'd been looking at the website for the funeral home. When I had found the obituary, I jumped back in the conversation.

Me: *It says here he died Sunday in Densmore. No services showing on the website.*

Bill: *Does it say if his mother is still living?*

Me: *There is no info at all.*

Karen: *Not sure, but I'm sending y'all the text I just got from my friend who works at the funeral home.*

The friend's text: *Hey, Karen. I have bad news but Bob Kilpatrick died Sunday. His body is here now.*

Bill: *I think I may call Ray Keller [a regional* Southern Gospel artist*] to see if he knows anything about this.*

Karen: *My friend says they aren't having any funeral or memorial service. His sister is having him cremated and that's it. This is so awful to me! I have no idea what happened to him. My friend said he'd let me know if he found out anything.*

Bill: *His brother's name is Donald. I wonder if $$$ is the reason for no service.*

Karen: *Maybe so, but he deserves a memorial service.*

Bill: *Um-hmm.*

Karen: *He's going to be promoting groups in Heaven now.*

By now you may have noticed that I had been rather quiet throughout all of this. That's because I was still looking at the obituary on the website—and something was starting to feel, *well*, odd. *Like,*

Densmore. That was quite a drive from where Bob lived and I had never known him to visit that area.

Back to the texts...

Me: *The date on the site puts him in his early 50s. Is that right?*

Bill: *I thought maybe he was closer to 60.*

Finally, I had to say it.

Me: *Ok, I have to ask ... is this the right Bob?*

Bill: *Come on ... is there another Bob Kilpatrick out there in this music?*

Karen: *Let me ask.*

Me: *I understand, Bill, but these hills are full of Kilpatricks. And it's kinda odd that not one group he worked with has not said anything. 'Course they may not know.*

Karen: *Here's another text from my friend at the funeral home.*

The friend's text: *It's definitely the promoter. The guys who brought the body in said it was. And, he looks just like what I remember when I was at concerts. Sort of sandy hair, but it's turned gray in most places ... not too tall, probably under six foot*

*... looks to be around 50-52. I found out he has a brother named Donald and a sister named Angela.*

Karen: *Guys, that has to be him. I know he's got a brother named Donald and a sister named Angela.*

Bill: *I remember meeting them. They were very nice to me.*

Karen: *Evidently it is the sister who is helping with the arrangements. But I sure do hate they're going just going to cremate him and not have any type of service.*

Have you ever been reading something and then all of sudden, something just clicked in your mind?

It was about this point, something clicked in mine—but I couldn't put my finger on what.

But meanwhile, the texts kept flying...

Bill: *I'm going to call Donald. Bob and Donald both live at their mom's house.*

Karen: *Let us know what he says.*

A few minutes go by.

Bill: *No answer or answering machine.*

Me: *I wonder what happened.*

Bill: *I wonder if The John Smith Singers might know anything. I'll call.*

Karen: *I wonder, too.*

Another few minutes.

Bill: *They didn't know about it but they said they'd make a few calls and let me know. They said they hadn't talked to Bob in a few months.*

Karen: *You know, I think his mom is still living. But she's been pretty sick, you know.*

*Two months ago, he dropped a box of videos and pictures at my friend's mom's house. He wanted her to have them. He was cleaning out his house since he didn't know where he would live after his mother passed away. He wanted my friend to have the stuff to give to her kids.*

Bill: *Interesting.*

Karen: *I wonder what happened. Maybe it was a heart attack. Guys, he's going to be promoting groups in Heaven now.*

Is there an echo?

The texts quieted down at this point. And then it hit me ... *"not too tall, probably under six foot."* Hmmm... probably under six foot. Wait! Bob stood more than 6 foot tall.

Then my mind instantly went back to Densmore—that was quite a drive from Bob's house. And, *"looks to be around 50-52."* Just as I was about to point this out...

Bill: *Hold the presses! It's not "our" Bob.*

Karen: *Whhhhaaaattt??? The funeral home said it was!*

Me: *I'm getting ready to laugh.*

Karen: *Y'allllllllllll...*

Bill: *That group called back and said they had talked to a friend of theirs who had talked with Bob just last night.*

Karen: *I'm now having mixed emotions. I do not want him dead but...Y'all will never let me live this down!*

Me: *I* AM *laughing now.*

Bill: *Hahaha!*

Karen: *But the guy who owns the funeral said he had the body!*

Bill: *Hmm...*

Karen: *Ok, I'm laughing out loud now. I'm dying.*

Me: *No, you're not really dying. We won't believe you now if you were anyway. You gonna promote groups in Heaven?*

Karen: *I'm calling the funeral home right now.*

Bill: *Thank the Lord for cell phones and text messages. I wouldn't have missed the last 30 minutes for anything!*

Me: *You know, if this turns out to be someone from China or Mexico...*

Bill: *Ha!*

A few moments of silence and then...

Karen: *I just got off the phone. My friend is calling the owner of the funeral home right now. Stay tuned. They still think it's our Bob.*

Me: *But they said this guy was around 50.*

Karen: *Well, maybe he looks younger lying down.*

Yes, you read that right. Karen just said, "Well, maybe he looks younger lying down."

Bill: *Ha! Ha! Ha! You're now hoping it's him!*

Karen: *No!!!*

Me: *Ok, I'll just settle it all. Karen, get ready. We're going to the funeral home. I'll swing by the house and we'll just go ID the body.*

Karen: *LOL!*

A few seconds passed...

Karen: *Wait. Do you think we could?*

Bill: *Now I'm crying! I'm laughing so hard. These other pastors with me are looking at me like I'm crazy!*

Karen: *The guys who brought him in say they are sure it is Bob!*

Bill: *Well, they ought to know ... if he looks younger lying down. Ha!*

Karen: *I can see y'all aren't going to let me forget this. The funeral home is calling me. Be right back.*

A minute. Then two minutes. Then ten.

Karen: *After I hung with up with the funeral home, I just decided I'd call Bob's number myself.*

Me: *Well?*

Karen: *I called and talked with ... Bob. The first thing he said was, 'I'm NOT dead.'*

A few moments of silence (meaning Bill and I were laughing uncontrollably in two different locations while Karen was waiting on someone to respond. So...

Me: *Karen, if I ever get sick, DON'T TELL ANYONE!!!*

Karen: *Y'all CANNOT imagine how I felt when he answered the phone! First time I've ever talked with a dead man!*

The rest of the story... strange but true...

Apparently, in Densmore, there was a gentleman by the name of Bob Kilpatrick who had passed away on Sunday night. Just like "our" Bob, he had a brother named Donald and a sister named Angela. After Bob's death, Angela requested that the body be taken to the same funeral home that "our" Bob's family used for the memorial services of their relatives.

When the funeral directors arrived in Densmore to pick up Bob, they read the paperwork and saw the name. With a quick glance at the deceased, they saw just enough resemblance between that Bob and "our" Bob to make the assumption.

Upon arriving at the funeral home, they told one of the workers that this was Bob Kilpatrick—and one of those workers called Karen.

But apparently Karen wasn't the only one who was called. Remember how Bob answered with "I'm NOT dead!"? By the time Karen called him, Bob had already spent most of the afternoon telling people the deceased was not him!

As with every good story, there is a moral to be taken to heart. In this case, the moral is...

You might look younger if you're lying down!

## Chapter 21

# Be Encouraged

*Too many treasures are waiting over yonder... there's too much to gain to lose.*

The lyrics to that classic Dottie Rambo song have been coursing through my brain a lot in recent months. Maybe it's age, maybe it's just a phase in my life, or maybe it's a quiet comfort from above. Whatever the case, I've found myself using that very phrase when in deep discussion with some of my artist friends—not just on professional matters but on personal matters as well.

One thing I've learned in my 50 years is that while many people have the gift of encouragement, just as many have what I call the "gift" of discouragement. Some of those people are so effective at sharing their gift that I've seen many friends just throw up their hands and just want to walk away (justifiably, I might add). On a personal level I've thrown my hands up so much that I've probably dislocated my shoulder dozens of times.

But if we are truly called to be a part of Southern Gospel—or really just life in general—we have to realize that that discouragement is rooted in the forces of evil and we have to look beyond that discouragement. The Book of all books plainly shows the outcome of this thing called life and it is in that promise that we have to remember that there is indeed too much to gain to lose.

As I close this book, be encouraged! Home is not that far away! Be encouraged, knowing that a genuine compassionate smile is a slap to the face of a devil that has a miserable eternity. Be encouraged in knowing your voice of Godly reason shakes the very foundation of hell. Be encouraged as the trials of today are the triumphs of tomorrow. Just because you've turned 50...or 60...or 70...or 80...or 90...or more, there's still a lot of life to live. And because your life experience has given you great wisdom, you can be encouraged with the greatest knowledge of all...

*Yesterday, today, tomorrow, and forever, God is still God! And He loves us.*

.

CPSIA information can be obtained at www.ICGtesting.com
Printed in the USA
LVOW11s0241150716

496224LV00002B/3/P